SUMMARY OF LIVING YOUR LOVE STORY

Timeless Wisdom for Dating, Marriage, and Intimacy

PHIL HOPPER

DESTINY IMAGE

All emphasis within Scripture quotations is the author's own. Please note that Destiny Image's publishing style capitalizes certain pronouns in Scripture that refer to the Father, Son, and Holy Spirit, and may differ from some publishers' styles. Take note that the name satan and related names are not capitalized. We choose not to acknowledge him, even to the point of violating grammatical rules.

Destiny Image P.O. Box 310, Shippensburg, PA 17257-0310

This book and all other Destiny Image's books are available at Christian bookstores and distributors worldwide.

For Worldwide Distribution.

Reach us on the Internet: www.destinyimage.com.

ISBN 13 TP: 9798881504465

ISBN 13 eBook: 9798881504472

CONTENTS

INTRODUCTION

In "Living Your Love Story," we embark on an intimate journey through the ebbs and flows of a relationship that mirrors the timeless wisdom found in the Song of Solomon. This sacred text, renowned for its poetic and allegorical depiction of romantic love, serves as the foundation for exploring the profound and often complex nature of marital commitment and affection.

The essence of "Living Your Love Story" is to illuminate the paths that couples can walk to cultivate a love that not only endures but thrives against the backdrop of everyday challenges. Each chapter of the book delves into different stages of a relationship, from the initial sparks of attraction and the deepening of emotional bonds, to navigating conflicts, celebrating joys, and sustaining love through the changing seasons of life.

The Song of Solomon offers rich imagery and metaphorical insights that are dissected in this summary to provide readers with practical guidance on fostering a relationship that is deeply rooted in respect, understanding, and a commitment to mutual growth. The book is not just a narrative; it is a manual and a meditation on love as one of the most profound human experiences.

By drawing parallels between the ancient text and modern relationships, "Living Your Love Story" invites readers to reflect on their own love lives and to rediscover the passion and connection that may be dormant but is always capable of revival. Through engaging explanations and actionable advice, the book encourages readers to view their relationships through a lens of intentional love and deliberate action.

This summary aims to encapsulate the key teachings and insights from "Living Your Love Story," offering a condensed version of its wisdom that is both accessible and compelling. It is designed for anyone who seeks to deepen their understanding of love as both a spiritual and practical journey, ensuring that every reader can find value, whether they are in the flush of new love, the depths of a long-term commitment, or anywhere in between.

Join us as we explore the essence of what it means to live out your love story, not just as a series of happenings but as a conscious, deliberate act of choosing love, every day, in every way. This journey is not just about staying in love, but about growing in love, and this summary provides the tools and insights necessary to navigate this beautiful, lifelong quest.

CHAPTER 1

TIME TO DEFINE THE RELATIONSHIP

Bible Verse

John 10:11 – "I am the good shepherd. The good shepherd lays down his life for the sheep."

Introduction

In this chapter, the author shares a personal story from his youth, involving a budding romance during his college years, to illustrate a deeper message about defining our most crucial relationship: the one with Jesus Christ. The narrative intertwines his romantic life with spiritual insights, emphasizing the need to commit fully to Jesus, much like in a marriage.

Word of Wisdom

"Jesus is pursuing you. He is a hopeless romantic who loves you so much that He freely gave His life for you." Phil Hopper

. . .

Main Theme

The main theme of this chapter revolves around the importance of commitment, both in human relationships and, more importantly, in our relationship with Jesus. It draws parallels between earthly courtship leading to marriage and a spiritual commitment to Christ.

Key Points

- The author recalls a pivotal moment in his college life where he risked his football scholarship for love, paralleling this personal risk with the ultimate sacrifice made by Jesus.
- Jesus is portrayed as the eternal Bridegroom, who pursues His bride (the Church) with a sacrificial love, reflecting the profound biblical motif of divine love.
- The historical and cultural context of marriage and purity are explored through the lens of Solomon's story from the Bible, emphasizing themes of redemption and forgiveness.
- The author stresses the dangers of rejecting Jesus' pursuit, highlighting the biblical principle that continual rejection of Christ can lead to spiritual abandonment.
- Commitment in relationships, especially in dating and marriage, is discussed, urging young people to define their

relationships clearly and commit wholeheartedly.
- The narrative concludes with a personal reflection on how the author's life was profoundly shaped by reciprocating Christa's love, drawing a parallel to how our lives are transformed when we commit to Jesus.

Key Themes

- **Risk and Sacrifice in Love**: The author's personal story of risking everything for love serves as a metaphor for the greater risk Jesus took for humanity. This illustrates the depth of commitment required in our relationship with Christ, urging us to consider what we are willing to risk for Him.
- **Biblical Parallels with Solomon**: Solomon's role as a shepherd and a king foreshadows Christ's relationship with His Church. The chapter draws comparisons between Solomon's earthly love story and Jesus' heavenly love story with us, emphasizing redemption and divine love.
- **Cultural Perspectives on Purity and Marriage**: Through the Shulamite woman's story, the chapter explores how societal views on beauty and purity have changed over time, and how these concepts relate to spiritual purity in Christianity.
- **Consequences of Rejection**: Discussing the severe consequences of continually rejecting Jesus' pursuit, the chapter warns

of a point where God may give individuals over to their desires, paralleling this with scriptural references from Romans.

- **The Importance of Defining Relationships**: The need to define earthly relationships clearly is used as an analogy for the clarity required in our commitment to Jesus. This theme is crucial for understanding the nature of our relationship with Christ as not just a savior but as a lifelong partner.
- **Transformation Through Love**: The transformative power of love, both human and divine, is a central theme. The author's life trajectory changed dramatically due to his romantic commitment, just as our spiritual paths are altered when we fully commit to Jesus.

Conclusion

The chapter compellingly urges readers to consider the seriousness of their relationship with Jesus Christ. It uses the metaphor of marriage to discuss the depth of commitment required in this divine relationship, emphasizing that just as in human relationships, half-heartedness has no place in our spiritual journey. It's a call to move from casual acquaintance to devoted commitment, reflecting on how defining our relationship with Jesus has eternal implications.

CHAPTER 2

THE BETROTHAL

Bible Verse

John 14:2-3 – "In My Father's house are many mansions; if it were not so, I would have told you. I go to prepare a place for you. And if I go and prepare a place for you, I will come again and receive you to Myself; that where I am, there you may be also."

Introduction

In this chapter, the author uses his son Jake's romantic proposal preparations as a springboard to delve into the profound and sacred rituals of ancient Jewish betrothal practices, comparing them to the Christian commitment to Jesus Christ. This narrative serves as a metaphor for our spiritual relationship with Christ, portraying Him as the ultimate Bridegroom preparing for our eternal union.

Word of Wisdom

"Jesus is not jealous of you—He is jealous for you." Phil Hopper

Main Theme

The main theme of this chapter is the sacredness and legality of the betrothal process in ancient Jewish culture, which symbolizes the Christian's spiritual betrothal to Jesus Christ. This spiritual engagement emphasizes preparation, promise, and purity as we await Jesus' return.

Key Points

- Jake's meticulous planning for his proposal mirrors the ancient Jewish betrothal process, highlighting the seriousness and sanctity of commitments.
- The Ketubah in Jewish tradition was a legally binding agreement that emphasized the purity and readiness of the bride for her groom.
- Ancient Jewish weddings were elaborate and symbolic, featuring a betrothal, a bridal chamber preparation, and a consummation, all reflective of our relationship with Christ.
- The chapter portrays Jesus as a Bridegroom who has gone to prepare a place for His bride, promising to return for her, similar to the Jewish groom.
- Christians are described as being in a betrothal stage with Christ, marked by

legal commitment, moral purity, and anticipatory preparation.

- The narrative warns against spiritual adultery, highlighting the seriousness with which we should honor our commitment to Christ.

Key Themes

- **Legal and Sacred Commitment**: The Ketubah represented a binding contract that not only outlined the responsibilities of both parties but also set the moral and legal framework for the marriage. This ancient contract mirrors the covenant relationship between Christians and Christ, where mutual promises of fidelity and commitment are central.
- **Preparation and Promise**: Just as the Jewish groom would leave to prepare the bridal chamber, Jesus promises to prepare a place for us in His Father's house, underscoring the theme of divine preparation and promise that sustains the believer's hope and purity.
- **Purity and Anticipation**: The ancient Jewish bride was expected to maintain her purity and readiness, living in anticipation of her groom's return. This mirrors the Christian's call to live a life of holiness, set apart for when Christ returns.
- **Symbolism of the Wedding Stages**: Each stage of the Jewish wedding—from betrothal to consummation—serves as a

profound metaphor for the Christian's journey with Christ, emphasizing the transition from promise to fulfillment.

- **Jealousy and Exclusivity**: The author uses the metaphor of human jealousy in marriage to illustrate Christ's desire for His followers' exclusive devotion. This challenges believers to forsake spiritual adultery and commit wholeheartedly to Him.

Conclusion

This chapter enriches the understanding of Christian commitment through the lens of ancient Jewish betrothal and wedding rituals. It calls for a heartfelt examination of our fidelity to Christ, urging us to live in purity and readiness for His return. As the Bride of Christ, we are encouraged to maintain our commitment, looking forward to the ultimate fulfillment of His promises when we are united with Him forever. The author's insights challenge us to consider our current spiritual state and realign our hearts toward Christ, our eternal Bridegroom.

CHAPTER 3

SINGLE, SATISFIED, AND READY

Bible Verse

1 Corinthians 7:27 – "Are you bound to a wife? Do not seek to be loosed. Are you loosed from a wife? Do not seek a wife."

Introduction

This chapter emphasizes the importance of finding contentment in singleness through a relationship with Christ, paralleling the single status of Solomon and his young maiden at the beginning of Song of Solomon. It challenges the misconception that marriage will complete one's happiness and instead positions Christ as the ultimate source of fulfillment.

Word of Wisdom

"Christ alone has the power to complete you." Phil Hopper

Main Theme

The theme of this chapter is the exploration of true contentment in singleness, arguing that such contentment is foundational and should not be dependent on marital status. It asserts that a complete and fulfilled life is achievable through a personal relationship with Jesus Christ, irrespective of whether one is single or married.

Key Points

- True contentment is found not in marital status but in one's relationship with Christ.
- The cultural ideal that marriage completes an individual is a misconception; true completion comes only from Christ.
- Singleness offers unique opportunities for spiritual growth and service that are distinct from married life.
- Biblical figures like Paul and Solomon serve as examples of how singleness can be fully embraced and used for God's purposes.
- Pursuing a spouse should not be about filling a void but about enhancing one's ability to serve God together.
- The choice between marriage and singleness should be guided by one's spiritual convictions and God's direction.

Key Themes

- **Contentment in Singleness**: The author underscores that contentment should be deeply rooted in Christ's love and not in a human relationship. True satisfaction comes from understanding and accepting Christ's unconditional love, which surpasses any human connection.

- **Myth of Completion through Marriage**: The societal belief that a partner can complete an individual is challenged; instead, the author points to Christ as the only one who can fulfill and complete a person's life. This spiritual completeness is what prepares one for a healthy, non-competitive marriage if it occurs.
- **Biblical Perspective on Singleness and Marriage**: Paul's teachings and the story of Solomon are cited to show that both singleness and marriage are respected states with distinct roles in Christian life. Each has its own challenges and blessings, and neither is inherently superior.
- **Practical Guidance for Single Christians**: The author provides practical advice for single Christians on dating and relationships, encouraging them to maintain standards, embrace humility, and seek God's will in their decisions.
- **Preparation for Potential Marriage**: While promoting contentment in singleness, the chapter also addresses how singles can prepare for marriage, should it be part of their future. It emphasizes the importance of personal growth, godly character, and spiritual readiness.

Conclusion

The chapter provides a comprehensive look at how singles can live fulfilled Christian lives. It emphasizes that whether one remains single or gets married, the key to contentment lies in a deep, personal relationship with Jesus Christ. By focusing on spiritual growth and readiness, singles can lead rich, purposeful lives, contributing uniquely to God's kingdom. The chapter ends by encouraging singles to embrace their status not as a period of waiting but as a time of active engagement in God's work.

CHAPTER 4
PATIENT AND PASSIONATE

Bible Verse

Ephesians 5:32 – "This is a great mystery, but I speak concerning Christ and the church."

Introduction

This chapter explores the sacredness of marriage and sexual relationships as divine metaphors for the union between Christ and His Church. It emphasizes the importance of patience and purity before marriage, drawing parallels with the marital preparation shown in Song of Solomon.

Word of Wisdom

"Our obedience toward God always brings the blessing of God." Phil Hopper

Main Theme

The chapter emphasizes the sanctity of marriage as a reflection of the spiritual union between Christ and the Church, advocating for sexual purity and integrity in the lead-up to marriage.

Key Points

- Marriage is designed by God as an unbreakable bond, reflecting the union between Christ and the Church.
- Sexual relationships within marriage are sacred and meant to signify our spiritual unity with Christ.
- The anticipation and passion in the Song of Solomon underscore the importance of patience and timing in romantic relationships.
- Premarital purity is crucial, as sexual intimacy before marriage goes against God's design and disrupts the spiritual metaphor.
- Patience in developing physical intimacy reflects wisdom and honors the sanctity of the marriage covenant.

Key Themes

- **Sacredness of Marriage**: The chapter asserts that marriage is a holy covenant designed by God to be lifelong and unbreakable, symbolizing the committed relationship between Christ and His

Church. This covenant is foundational, shaping the Christian approach to marriage and emphasizing its indissolubility.

- **Sexual Purity and Integrity**: It discusses the importance of maintaining sexual purity before marriage, likening premarital sexual relations to sin that tarnishes the divine reflection intended through marriage. The text encourages singles and couples to uphold purity as a form of obedience to God, promising divine blessings in return.
- **Metaphorical Significance of Marriage**: By drawing on Paul's teachings in Ephesians, the chapter highlights that the physical union in marriage is not merely an act of love between two people but a profound metaphor for the spiritual union between Christ and His followers. This perspective elevates the meaning and purpose of marital intimacy.
- **Challenges of Premarital Temptation**: The narrative cautions against the awakening of love before the appropriate time, using the allegory from Song of Solomon to illustrate the potential pitfalls of premature romantic escalation, which can lead to sin and spiritual discord.
- **Preparation for Marriage**: The discussion extends beyond the avoidance of sin, suggesting that couples engage in thoughtful, intentional preparation for marriage. This preparation involves setting boundaries, fostering mutual respect, and

cultivating a relationship centered on Christ.

Conclusion

"Patient and Passionate" provides a theological and practical framework for understanding marriage as a divine institution meant to mirror the sacred relationship between Christ and the Church. It advocates for patience and purity, emphasizing that these virtues not only comply with God's commandments but also enrich the marital relationship. The chapter calls for a deliberate approach to romance that honors God's timing, encouraging readers to reflect Christ's love in their relationships and uphold His standards in anticipation of marital bliss.

CHAPTER 5

MORE THAN A FEELING

Bible Verse

1 Corinthians 13:4-7 – "Love is patient, love is kind. It does not envy, it does not boast, it is not proud. It does not dishonor others, it is not self-seeking, it is not easily angered, it keeps no record of wrongs."

Introduction

This chapter underscores that love transcends mere feelings and requires deliberate, intentional actions to foster and maintain a lasting relationship. It explores the journey from dating to marriage, emphasizing intentional steps to ensure a healthy, lifelong union.

Word of Wisdom

"Falling in love is easy; staying in love is your choice." Phil Hopper

Main Theme

The main theme emphasizes that true love in relationships, especially in marriage, goes beyond initial feelings of infatuation to include intentional, thoughtful actions that cultivate a deep, enduring bond.

Key Points

- Love is an intentional act beyond just feelings.
- Dating should be approached with the goal of marriage in mind, not as a casual endeavor.
- Emotional and spiritual maturity is crucial for handling romantic relationships responsibly.
- Healthy relationships begin with self-awareness and intentionality in dating.
- Infatuation must evolve into a deeper, intentional love to last.
- Intentional dating involves progressing through stages deliberately: dating with intention, courtship, engagement, and marriage.

Key Themes

- **Intentional Dating and Courtship**: The chapter explains that dating should be purposeful with the end goal of marriage. This approach helps prevent the common cycle of relationship turnover seen in modern dating practices, promoting a more stable foundation for future marriage.

- **Emotional and Spiritual Maturity**: It is vital to assess one's emotional and spiritual readiness before entering into a relationship. This maturity influences the health of the relationship, helping to ensure that both partners are prepared for the commitment and challenges of a lifelong union.
- **The Transition from Infatuation to Love**: Initially, relationships often begin with infatuation, but transitioning to love requires intentional actions and decisions. True love is nurtured through mutual respect, understanding, and shared values, not merely sustained by feelings.
- **Role of Family in Relationships**: Understanding and integrating into each other's family is crucial as it offers insights into the partner's background and values. This integration is part of the courtship process that solidifies the bond and alignment in the relationship.
- **Navigating Challenges in Relationships**: The chapter discusses how to handle inevitable challenges in relationships, including differences in belief systems and life goals. Successful navigation of these challenges through communication and compromise is essential for a healthy relationship.

Conclusion

"More than a Feeling" delivers a profound message on the necessity of intentional actions in cultivating and sustaining love. It clarifies that while falling in love might be effortless, maintaining that love requires consistent, deliberate effort and choices that align with a shared future vision. The chapter encourages readers to approach relationships with maturity, intentionality, and a clear understanding of the work involved in building a lasting bond.

CHAPTER 6

HIS NEEDS; HER NEEDS

Bible Verse

Ephesians 5:33 – "Nevertheless let each one of you in particular so love his own wife as himself, and let the wife see that she respects her husband."

Introduction

This chapter delves into the unique emotional needs of men and women, illustrating how understanding and addressing these needs are crucial for a deep and fulfilling marital relationship. It draws from the Biblical narrative of Solomon and the Shulamite to explore themes of love, respect, and mutual fulfillment.

Word of Wisdom

"Men and women fall out of love when their emotional accounts become overdrawn." Phil Hopper

Main Theme

The main theme centers on recognizing and fulfilling the distinct emotional needs of men and women in marriage, which is essential for sustaining deep intimacy and happiness.

Key Points

- Men and women, though equal, have different emotional needs.
- Understanding and meeting these needs is crucial for marital happiness.
- Emotional deposits enhance love; withdrawals can deplete it.
- True intimacy encompasses emotional, spiritual, and mental connection.
- Addressing each other's needs prevents misunderstanding and disappointment.
- Biblical principles can guide couples in nurturing a lasting relationship.

Key Themes

- **Understanding Gender-Specific Needs**: Men and women have inherently different ways they experience and express love. Men typically crave respect and admiration, which makes them feel valued, while women desire affection and reassurance of their worth and beauty.
- **Emotional Deposits and Withdrawals**: Just like a bank account, relationships have emotional reserves that

can be filled or depleted. Positive interactions act as deposits, strengthening love, while negative interactions are withdrawals, potentially leading to emotional bankruptcy.

- **The Role of Intimacy in Marriage**: Intimacy in marriage is not limited to physical closeness but extends to emotional, spiritual, and intellectual connections. This broader understanding of intimacy can lead to a more satisfying and resilient marriage.
- **Cultural Misunderstandings of Gender Roles**: Society often blurs the distinctive qualities of men and women, which can lead to conflicts in understanding and meeting each other's needs. Acknowledging and valuing these differences can lead to greater marital harmony.
- **Practical Steps to Meeting Spousal Needs**: The chapter provides actionable advice for husbands and wives on how to continually meet each other's core emotional needs through respect, admiration, affection, and understanding, fostering a cycle of mutual satisfaction and deepening love.

Conclusion

"His Needs; Her Needs" emphasizes the importance of recognizing and addressing the specific needs of spouses in a marriage. By understanding the unique ways men and women perceive love and appreciation, couples can foster a more intimate and enduring relationship. The chapter encourages couples to actively invest in their emotional connection, using biblical wisdom to guide their interactions and ensure a fulfilling marital bond.

CHAPTER 7

MORE THAN MEETS THE EYE

Bible Verse

Matthew 26:27-28 – "Then He took the cup, gave thanks, and gave it to them, saying, 'Drink from it, all of you. For this is My blood of the new covenant, which is shed for many for the remission of sins.'"

Introduction

In Song of Solomon chapter 3, the narrative transitions into the sacred union of marriage, symbolizing the profound covenant between Christ and His Church. This chapter explores the rich symbolism of marriage in the Christian faith, portraying it as a divine reflection of Jesus's sacrificial love for humanity.

Word of Wisdom

"Every time you take communion and drink from that cup, you say, 'I'm in

covenant with Jesus as my Bridegroom."[iii]
Phil Hopper

Main Theme

The main theme of this chapter is the depiction of marriage as a divine covenant that mirrors Christ's relationship with the Church, highlighting the deep spiritual significance and commitments embodied in this union.

Key Points

• Marriage is a divine institution that reflects Christ's love for the Church.

• The Hebrew wedding customs provide a deeper understanding of Jesus's covenant with His people.

• Communion symbolizes accepting the covenant with Jesus, akin to a bride accepting a marriage proposal.

• Preparation for marital union in the Bible parallels Christians preparing for Christ's return.

• Marriage serves both sanctification and satisfaction within a Christian's life.

• The ultimate union in marriage reflects the unity of the Trinity and the believer's relationship with Christ.

Key Themes

- **Biblical Foundations of Marriage**: The covenant of marriage in Christian doctrine is not just about companionship and love but serves as a profound symbol of Christ's covenant with the Church, emphasizing how sacred vows reflect deeper spiritual truths.
- **Symbolism of Hebrew Wedding Traditions**: Understanding ancient Hebrew wedding customs enriches the Christian perspective on Jesus's promises and His sacrificial love, with rituals like the bridal cup of wine during communion echoing Christ's commitment to His followers.
- **Sanctification Through Marriage**: Marriage is portrayed not merely as a path to personal happiness but as a journey of sanctification, where spouses learn to embody Christ's love and sacrifice, mirroring His sanctifying work on the Church.
- **Anticipation of Christ's Return**: Just as a bride anticipates her groom's return, Christians are to prepare spiritually for Christ's second coming, living in a state of readiness and purity, reflecting the bridal preparations in ancient Jewish customs.
- **Marriage as a Reflection of the Trinity**: The marital union is depicted as a mirror of the Trinity, where the husband and wife's roles reflect the relational dynamics within the Godhead, emphasizing unity and mutual submission.

Conclusion

"More than Meets the Eye" elevates the understanding of marriage from a mere social or romantic arrangement to a sacred covenant that encapsulates the essence of Christian theology. It underscores the depth of commitment, preparation, and divine purpose in the marital bond, drawing parallels with Christ's eternal covenant with His Church. This chapter not only deepens the understanding of marital roles but also enhances the appreciation of communion and the anticipatory nature of Christian life awaiting Christ's return.

CHAPTER 8

SACRED AND SIZZLING SEX

Bible Verse

Hebrews 13:4 – "Marriage is honorable among all, and the bed undefiled; but fornicators and adulterers God will judge."

Introduction

This chapter delves into the sacred aspect of sex within marriage, contrasting God's purpose for sexual intimacy with the distorted views prevalent in today's society. It underscores the sanctity and enjoyment of sexual relations between married couples as intended by God, opposing both the permissive and repressive extremes seen in modern culture.

Word of Wisdom

"Every time you take communion and drink from that cup, you say, 'I'm in

covenant with Jesus as my Bridegroom."'
Phil Hopper

Main Theme

The main theme of this chapter is the celebration of sex within the confines of marriage as both a sacred act ordained by God and a source of joy and intimacy for couples, countering cultural misconceptions and highlighting its role in a healthy marital relationship.

Key Points

• Sex is sacred and meant to be enjoyed within the bounds of marriage.

• Cultural misconceptions about sex lead to harm and confusion.

• God's boundaries on sex are protective, not restrictive.

• The distortion of sexual values has severe societal repercussions.

• Marriage allows for a healthy, joyous expression of sexual love.

• Misunderstandings within the church about sex need correction.

Key Themes

- **Distinction between Sacred and Profane Views**: The chapter emphasizes that while society often treats sex as casual and inconsequential, in Christianity, it is a sacred union that mirrors Christ's relationship with the Church, intended to strengthen marital bonds and reflect divine love.

- **Consequences of Cultural Misconceptions**: It discusses the detrimental effects of both hyper-sexualization and repressive attitudes towards sex in society, leading to issues like sexual abuse, addiction, and unhealthy views about intimacy and relationships.
- **Biblical Sanctity of Marital Sex**: This theme explores the scriptural basis for sex as a gift from God to married couples, meant to be enjoyed and revered, challenging both libertine and overly restrictive cultural norms.
- **Restoration and Healing**: The chapter offers hope and guidance for those who have experienced harm or distortion in their understanding of sex, pointing to Jesus's healing as a path to reclaiming and enjoying sex as God intended.
- **Practical Advice for Marital Intimacy**: It provides practical tips for deepening intimacy through communication, understanding, and mutual respect, emphasizing that sexual satisfaction in marriage grows from emotional and spiritual connection.

Conclusion

"Sacred and Sizzling Sex" advocates for a return to viewing sexual intimacy as a profound and delightful aspect of marital life, designed by God not only for procreation but for pleasure and deep connection between spouses. The chapter calls for a balanced approach that celebrates this gift, mitigates against cultural distortions, and fosters a fulfilling marital relationship.

CHAPTER 9

WHEN YOU'VE LOST THAT LOVIN' FEELIN'

Bible Verse

Ephesians 5:33 - "Nevertheless let each one of you in particular so love his own wife as himself, and let the wife see that she respects her husband."

Introduction

This chapter explores conflict in marriage, using Solomon and the Shulamite's experiences from Song of Solomon chapter 5 as a backdrop. It discusses the inevitability of conflict and the importance of healthy conflict resolution to maintain intimacy and mutual respect in marriage.

Word of Wisdom

"Stop fighting for your rights and start fighting for your marriage." Phil Hopper

Main Theme

The main theme focuses on navigating marital conflicts constructively. It emphasizes that conflict is a normal part of marriage and handling it well can strengthen the relationship rather than weaken it.

Key Points

• Conflict in marriage is inevitable and handling it well is crucial for a healthy relationship.

• Proper conflict resolution can prevent long-term damage and promote understanding and intimacy.

• Both partners should strive to understand and meet the other's needs rather than insisting on their own.

• Solomon's approach to marital conflict emphasizes patience, understanding, and humility.

• Effective conflict resolution requires mutual respect and love.

• The chapter uses Solomon and the Shulamite's story as an example to discuss broader marital issues.

Key Themes

- **Healthy Conflict Resolution**: The chapter highlights that the way couples handle conflict can define their marriage's health. Effective conflict resolution involves empathy, mutual respect, and a willingness to put the relationship above one's ego.

- **Mutual Responsibility and Submission**: It discusses the biblical concept of mutual submission in marriage, where both partners are responsible for each other's emotional and physical well-being, echoing the unity described in Ephesians.
- **Impact of Unresolved Conflicts**: Unresolved conflicts can lead to long-term dissatisfaction and emotional distance. Addressing conflicts promptly and constructively can prevent the erosion of intimacy.
- **Communication and Reconciliation**: The importance of communication in resolving conflicts is emphasized. Solomon's gentle approach to a marital spat is presented as a model for effective and loving communication.
- **Spiritual and Emotional Intimacy**: The chapter connects the resolution of marital conflicts with the deepening of spiritual and emotional intimacy, suggesting that navigating through difficulties together strengthens the marital bond.

Conclusion

"When You've Lost That Lovin' Feelin'" calls for a reevaluation of how conflicts are handled within marriage, urging couples to approach disagreements with a heart of service and love. By fostering an environment of mutual respect and understanding, marriages can thrive even in the face of inevitable challenges.

CHAPTER 10

HOW TO GET BACK THAT LOVIN' FEELIN'

Bible Verse

1 Peter 3:7 - "Husbands, likewise, dwell with them with understanding, giving honor to the wife, as to the weaker vessel, and as being heirs together of the grace of life, that your prayers may not be hindered."

Introduction

This chapter explores the journey of rekindling love in marriage, illustrating how couples can move from a place of conflict to one of renewed affection and deeper understanding through deliberate actions and choices.

Word of Wisdom

"Put your love into action, and you'll get back that lovin' feeling." Phil Hopper

Main Theme

The main theme revolves around the dynamic of falling out of love and the conscious effort required to reignite that love, emphasizing that love is both a feeling and an active choice.

Key Points

• Love is both an emotion and a motion; it requires action to sustain.

• Eros (romantic love) and agape (unconditional love) are both necessary in a marriage.

• Choosing to act lovingly can rekindle feelings of love.

• Conflicts are inevitable but can be resolved through understanding and humility.

• The reestablishment of love in marriage often requires returning to the foundational behaviors that initially built the relationship.

• Restored love follows deliberate, loving actions and choices within the marriage.

Key Themes

- **The Dual Nature of Love**: The chapter stresses that love in marriage encompasses both feelings and actions. While eros focuses on romantic attraction, agape involves choices that prioritize the partner's needs, creating a sustainable bond.

- **Reigniting Love Through Actions**: Actions speak louder than words in a marriage. By revisiting and replicating the initial loving actions that once sparked joy and affection, couples can rekindle their emotional connection.
- **The Role of Conflict in Marriage**: Conflict is portrayed not as a sign of failure but as an opportunity for growth and deeper intimacy. Effective management of disagreements strengthens marital bonds.
- **Importance of Understanding and Patience**: The story of Solomon and the Shulamite serves as a reminder of the importance of patience, understanding, and empathy in overcoming marital strife and fostering lasting love.
- **Transformative Power of Mutual Submission**: Mutual submission, rooted in humility and a service-oriented attitude towards one's spouse, is highlighted as a cornerstone for a thriving marriage, reflecting biblical teachings on marital roles.

Conclusion

"How to Get Back that Lovin' Feelin'" underscores that maintaining a loving marriage requires ongoing effort, understanding, and the willingness to act in love, even when feelings wane. By actively choosing to love and serve one another, couples can navigate through conflicts and challenges, ultimately strengthening their relationship for a lifetime of love and companionship.

CHAPTER 11
THE GARDENER

Bible Verse

Proverbs 5:18-19 - "Let your fountain be blessed, and rejoice in the wife of your youth. As a loving deer and a graceful doe, let her breasts satisfy you at all times; and always be enraptured with her love."

Introduction

This chapter delves into the mature stages of marriage as portrayed in Song of Solomon chapter 7, where Solomon reflects on the deepened beauty and virtue of his long-time wife, illustrating the gradual yet profound growth of love and admiration over time.

Word of Wisdom

"Every husband is called to be a gardener." Phil Hopper

Main Theme

The theme centers on the evolving nature of marital love, comparing it to a well-tended garden that flourishes over time through nurturing, dedication, and a deep appreciation for the enduring beauty that develops within a committed relationship.

Key Points

• Marital love matures and deepens over the years, much like a well-cultivated garden.

• True appreciation of a partner's beauty, both internal and external, grows with time.

• Solomon's poetic descriptions in Song of Solomon chapter 7 emphasize a shift from initial attraction to profound admiration.

• The metaphor of a gardener illustrates a husband's role in cultivating and nurturing the marital relationship.

• Deep intimacy and mutual trust are fundamental outcomes of diligently caring for one's marital "garden."

• Continuous effort in nurturing a marriage leads to the richest and most fulfilling stages of the relationship.

Key Themes

- **Progressive Recognition of Beauty**: Initially attracted to his wife's outward beauty, Solomon's descriptions transition to deeper, internal qualities as their marriage matures, highlighting a shift in perception from superficial allure to substantial and enduring traits.
- **Gardening as a Metaphor for Marriage**: Just as a gardener tends to his garden, ensuring its growth and protection, a husband is encouraged to actively nurture his marriage, emphasizing consistent effort and protective vigilance against potential threats.
- **Roles of Trust and Security**: By expressing unwavering trust and admiration for his wife's inner strength and virtues, Solomon sets a standard for marital trust, illustrating how deep security can fortify a loving relationship against external adversities.
- **Marital Intimacy Over Time**: The depth of marital intimacy is likened to the aging of fine wine, suggesting that the best and most satisfying aspects of a marriage can only emerge through sustained love, patience, and mutual nurturing.
- **Sustained Effort and Leadership in Marriage**: The chapter advocates for active, intentional leadership in marriage, where husbands are called to be the primary nurturers of the relationship, continuously working to maintain and enhance the marital bond.

Conclusion

"The Gardener" in Song of Solomon chapter 7 vividly captures the evolution of marital love from its initial stages to a profound, mature relationship full of admiration and deep connection. It reinforces the idea that like a garden, a successful marriage requires ongoing attention, dedication, and a heart for continual nurturing, yielding a bountiful, ever-enriching life partnership.

CHAPTER 12

Bible Verse

"So I prophesied as I was commanded; and as I prophesied, there was a noise, and suddenly a rattling; and the bones came together, bone to bone." (Ezekiel 37:7)

Introduction

Dr. Tim Hamon's 2018 message highlighted a pivotal moment for the prophetic movement—a call for a fresh "breath" or "ruach" to animate the body, moving beyond assembly and preparation to dynamic, Spirit-filled action.

Word of Wisdom

"We've been equipping, preparing, making strong, putting together, assembling together all those people and now we

want to be an army." - Emma Stark

Main Theme

The chapter discusses a prophesied "second wind" of the prophetic movement, emphasizing the need for a new spiritual breath to invigorate and mobilize the prophetic community into action.

Key Points

• Dr. Tim Hamon declared the start of a second prophetic wave at Christian International.

• Prophetic leaders have laid a foundation, but a fresh spiritual breath is needed.

• Key prophecies in 2016 from Barbara Yoder, Cindy Jacobs, Dutch Sheets, and Bishop Bill Hamon foresaw this new wave.

• The second wave calls for prophetic action, not just preparation and assembly.

• This new phase is characterized by a "second wind" necessary for prophetic revival and authority.

• The second wave will build upon previous efforts but venture into new territories with fresh understanding.

Key Themes

- **Honoring Pioneers:** Respect and gratitude for those who pioneered the prophetic movement is vital. Their struggles to normalize prophetic ministry set the stage for the next wave.

- **New Purity:** The second wave demands a higher standard of purity, eschewing ego, religious control, and political spirits. A full embrace of Jeremiah 1:10's mandate to build and plant is required.
- **Echoing God Faithfully:** Second wave prophets must accurately reflect the breadth of God's character, avoiding personal biases and embracing the role of "echo" rather than originator.
- **Fresh Revelation Required:** Prophets must seek continual intimacy with God to gain fresh insight and avoid stale, repeated revelations.
- **Strong Challenge and Accountability:** The new wave will challenge prophets to speak difficult truths with courage, ensuring they are held accountable and avoid complacency.

Conclusion

The second wave of the prophetic movement heralds a period of intensified spiritual activity and deeper intimacy with God. Prophets are called to rise above past limitations, echoing the fullness of God's character, and to move forward with renewed boldness and purity. This new chapter requires a strong community that honors its roots while eagerly stepping into its destiny with expectant hearts and ready spirits.

DESTINY IMAGE

Destiny Image is a prophetic Christian publisher dedicated to empowering believers through Spirit-led messages. Our mission is to equip and inspire individuals to fulfill their God-given destinies by providing transformative resources that resonate with the Charismatic and Pentecostal faith.

We specialize in books, blogs, and back cover copies that reflect prophetic insights, dynamic teachings, and testimonies of faith. Our commitment to fostering spiritual growth and kingdom impact makes Destiny Image a beacon for those seeking to deepen their relationship with God and embrace their calling in the power of the Holy Spirit.

www.ingramcontent.com/pod-product-compliance
Lightning Source LLC
Chambersburg PA
CBHW050814160726
48004CB00002B/837